# THE BOOK OF *323*
# NO TO TRUMP
## BUMPERSTICKERS

# THE BOOK OF *323*
# NO TO TRUMP
## BUMPERSTICKERS

## JOHN WIRTH

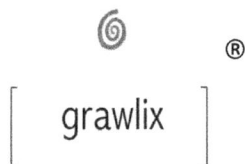

®

[ grawlix ]

Published September 2016 by
grawlix®
in USA

# DEDICATION

This book is dedicated to

# Mr. Donald J. Trump

for offering himself up as an object
of disapproval, contempt, derision and amusement

and for forcefully demonstrating by his words and deeds
that in political affairs
things can go suddenly, horribly bad

# I

According to Wikipedia, Donald John Trump (born June 14, 1946)
is an American businessman, television personality, author,
politician, Republican Party nominee
for President of the United States
and major asshole

# 2

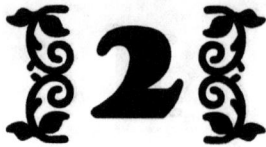

TRUMP SAYS HE WILL DEMAND
THAT ALL FOREIGN POLICIES
BE TRANSLATED INTO ENGLISH

# 3

TRUMP SAYS HE WILL ORDER THE ARMY
TO DE-CODE CHINA'S COMPUTER CODE

# 14

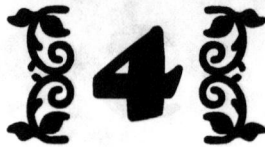

They tried to make a Manchurian candidate
out of Trump but they couldn't find a brain to wash

# 5

They're all about WINNING! Trump & Charlie Sheen
Now aren't they a pair?

# 6

A horse drops a dump
The Republican Party dropped a Trump

# 7

William F. Buckley said
Trump is a narcissist and a demagogue.
That about nails it.

# 8

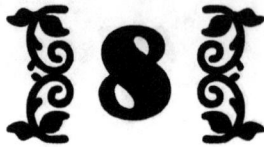

Gee, if you're a Republican
and the great William F. Buckley didn't like you,
where does that leave you?

# 9

THE REPUBLICAN BASE: OFF BASE

# 10

Trump:
Not only would be a disaster, IS a disaster

# 11

TRUMP TRUMP

# 12

LET THIS SERVE
AS EVIDENCE TO FUTURE HISTORIANS
THERE WAS RESISTANCE

# 13

MY GOD, WHO'S NEXT IN LINE
AFTER REAGAN AND TRUMP?
PEE-WEE HERMAN?

# 14

My god! This guy's *WORSE THAN NIXON!!*

# 15

TRUMP'S REAL NAME IS DRUMPF
HIS REAL GAME IS BULLSHIT

# 16

TRUSTING YOUR COUNTRY TO TRUMP
IS LIKE TRUSTING YOUR PORTFOLIO TO MADOFF

# 17

Now, if Trump were only clever
all would be forgiven

# 18

TRUMP: ENTERTAINING, INDEED—
BUT LESS SO THAN HOMER SIMPSON

# 19

TRUMP TRUMPETS. CLARABELL HONKED.
THE QUALITY OF COMMUNICATION IS EQUAL.

# 20

TRUMP COMES FROM GOOD STOCK
HIS GRANDFATHER WAS ALSO A DRAFT DODGER

# 21

FIRE CANDIDATE TRUMP

# 22

Trump likes Putin, Gaddafi, Napoleon . . .
How he does get off
on kinky dictators into uniforms

# 23

Trump is gay. His lover is himself.

# 24

Trump is gay. His lover is Mitch McConnell.

# 25

Trump doesn't need you to love him.
He's got himself.

# 26

Is it possible to be a more repugnant person than Donald J. Trump?
Hint: no

# 27

TRUMP'S DEVELOPMENTAL DELAY IS INFINITE

# 28

DONALD TRUMP IS THE ONLY PERSON IN THE WORLD
WHO THINKS DONALD TRUMP
IS AS HE ADVERTISES HIMSELF

# 29

Donald Trump's idea of hard work:
eating more than three pussies in a day

# 30

Donald Trump says he'd like to fuck his daughter
if she weren't his daughter.
His daughter says she would like to fuck her father
if he weren't an idiot.

# 31

Trump: It is to America's eternal embarrassment that it has to be confronted with this dork

# 32

To America's great redneck class:
if you think Donald Trump is not going
to fuck you over you'd best think again

# 33

I like Trump. He makes you feel good
while fucking you over.

# 34

American democracy has come to the point
of voting for the most revolting person
in the room. Live with it.

# 35

Retard as President. Get used to it?

# 36

What's the difference between Trump and piss?
Trump's face is yellower.

# 37

TRUMP'S SUNTAN: FAKE
EVERYTHING ELSE TRUMP: FAKE

# 38

TRUMP GIVES NEW MEANING
TO THE WORD MORON
AND A LOT OF OTHER WORDS . . .

# 39

CHRISTIE LIKES TRUMP
CHRIST DOESN'T

# 40

YEAH, BUT THEY DIDN'T
NOMINATE BARNUM FOR PRESIDENT

# 41

If it looks like an idiot and sounds like an idiot
it is a Donald Trump

# 42

Trump likes to put his name on everything
He'd tattoo it on his cock, if there was room

# 43

ONE IS JUST TOTALLY ASTONISHED AT HOW BAD
THIS GUY IS

# 44

TRUMP. REPUBLICANS, LIVE WITH IT.

# 45

IF TRUMP WINS, GOVERNMENT
BECOMES COMEDY.
AND TRAGEDY.

# 46

TO THINK THAT ALL OF AMERICAN HISTORY
COMES DOWN TO THIS DUMBASS

# 47

Trump: I can't get around how many people
voted for this guy

# 48

TRUMP IS INAPPROPRIATE

# 49

TRUMP DOESN'T USE A TELEPROMPTER
HE CAN'T READ

# 50

EVANGELICALS LOVE TRUMP
TRUMP LOVES EVANGELICALS—WITH BIG TITS

# 51

TRUMP DOES NOT HATE BLACKS.
TRUMP LOVES BLACKS
—WITH BIG ASSES

# 52

TRUMP DOES NOT HATE HISPANICS
TRUMP LOVES HISPANICS
—WITH A BRAZILIAN WAX

# 53

I LOVE TRUMP
HE'S NOT SMARTER THAN ME IN ANY WAY

# 54

HOW THE FUCK DID IT COME TO THIS?

# 55

WELL, WE DIDN'T DO SO WELL BY
"THE BEST AND THE BRIGHTEST"
SO NOW WE'RE GOING WITH
"THE WORST AND THE DUMBEST"?

# 56

TRUMP'S WORD IS AS GOOD AS HIS BOND
—JUNK BOND

# 57

What is so astonishing is that it is ever necessary to point out Trump's infinite vulgarity

# 58

TRUMP:
HEY, MY GOD, THIS AIN'T THE MAN

# 59

Trump is without embarrassment
but I certainly am not

# 60

THINGS __ARE__ RIGGED AGAINST TRUMP:
CIVILITY, DECENCY, COURTESY

# 61

GOD BROKE THE MOLD
BEFORE HE CREATED DONALD TRUMP

# 62

TRUMP HAS A PECULIAR AVERSION TO
CONSIDERATION FOR OTHERS

# 63

TRUMP WILL TAKE US IN A NEW DIRECTION
STRAIGHT DOWN

# 64

TRUMP LOVES FAMILY VALUES
TRUMP LOVES MARRIAGE
AS MANY TIMES AS POSSIBLE

# 65

IF TRUMP WINS HE WILL BE SWORN IN
ON A BIBLE THAT HAS NEVER BEEN OPENED

# 66

MAYBE THERE ARE MORE SENSIBLE AMERICANS
THAN WE THINK
(BUT PROBABLY NOT)

# 67

WHAT THE DONALD IS UP AGAINST:
IN AMERICA A POLITICIAN IS NOT SUPPOSED
TO BE NASTY

# 68

He walks like a duck, he squawks like a duck.
Must be The Donald is a duck.
Donald Duck.
"President Donald Duck."
Whoa.

# 69

AS IF THE WORLD WERE NOT FILLED
WITH ENOUGH MISERY
WE HAVE DONALD J. TRUMP
RUNNING FOR PRESIDENT

# 70

IT'S THE DONALD, STUPID!

# 71

TRUMP IS NOT A MISOGYNIST
HE LIKES PUSSY

# 72

MY IDEA OF HELL:
HAVING TO LISTEN ETERNALLY TO TRUMP TALK

# 73

TRUMP SAYS HE HAS NEVER SEEN ANY OF HIS WIVES SHIT
HE HASN'T SEEN ANY OF THEM LOOK IN HIS WALLET EITHER

# 74

LIES PASS THE LIPS OF TRUMP
AS EASILY AS VOMIT PASSES THE LIPS OF A BULIMIC

# 75

I'm trying to think of something bad you can say
about a person that doesn't apply to Donald Trump . . .
Give me a few minutes . . .

# 76

HEY, POOR WHITE MALE
NO WAY I'M VOTING TRUMP
LIVE WITH IT

## 77

YOU WON'T BE ABLE
TO COMPLAIN TO US
IF YOU VOTE FOR THE ANUS

# 78

> The best part of Donald Trump ran down his mother's leg.—old army adage

# 79

To expect Donald Trump
to say anything coherent
is to expect a cockroach to philosophize

# 80

DONALD TRUMP'S BRAIN IS A COMPUTER
THAT DOES NOT SUPPORT THE APP OF THOUGHT

# 81

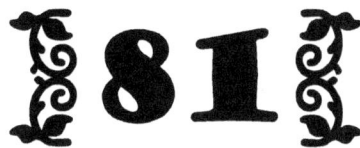

What is the definition of an asshole?
The dictionary definition of an asshole is:
"a person who in any respect
resembles Donald J. Trump"

# 82

TRUMP: HOW CAN A PERSON
WITH SUCH A SMALL BRAIN
HAVE SUCH A BIG HEAD?

# 83

TRUMP HAS GOT TO BE A DEMOCRAT MOLE

## 84

TRUMP SAYS THAT <u>HIS</u> VIETNAM WAR WAS AVOIDING STDS
SO IT COULDN'T BE SYPHILIS THAT HAS DESTROYED HIS BRAIN

# 85

WITH TRUMP, ALZHEIMER'S
WOULD BE AN IMPROVEMENT

# 86

When future geologists dig down
to the 2016 level
they will find a thick worldwide stratum
of fossilized Trump bullshit

# 87

TRUMP SHITS IN HIS THINKING CAP
SINCE HE CAN'T FIGURE OUT WHAT ELSE
TO DO WITH IT

**88**

Trump says he's got a plan to eliminate the national debt.
He's going to have the country declare bankruptcy.
Hey, it's worked for him.

## 89

TRUMP USES THE LADIES ROOM
BECAUSE THEY HAVE BIGGER MIRRORS

# 90

What an insult to our society is
Trump's presence in its midst!

# 91

THE SMELL OF FRAUD FOLLOWS TRUMP
LIKE A PARTICULARLY MALODOROUS FART

# 92

HOW LONG, O GOD! MUST WE SUFFER
THIS MAN!

# 93

IF TRUMP WERE TO MEET JESUS
HE WOULD TRY TO SELL HIM
AN OVERPRICED CONDO

# 94

TRUMP: NOT ONLY AN UNCERTAIN TRUMPET
BUT A BLEATING ONE

# 95

Oi veh! dat Donald poyson, vhat a shyster!

# 96

WHERE DID TRUMP'S MOM AND POP
GO SO TERRIBLY WRONG?

# 97

TRUMP IS A GENIUS—AT CHEATING

# 98

Trump's abuse of Government: forgivable.
Trump's abuse of Sensibility: not forgivable.

# 99

JOSEPH R. MCCARTHY: ADDICTED TO ALCOHOL
DONALD J. TRUMP: ADDICTED TO HIMSELF

# 100

GIVING TRUMP THE POWER OF THE PRESIDENCY
IS LIKE GIVING A FOUR-YEAR-OLD
THE KEYS TO YOUR CAR

# 101

IS TRUMP SOME KIND
OF FAILED GENETIC EXPERIMENT?

# 102

FOREIGN TO TRUMP'S EXPERIENCE:
CAREFUL CONSIDERATION

# 103

TRUMP DESTROYS THE AMERICAN EMPIRE: OK
TRUMP DESTROYS CIVILIZED BEHAVIOR: NOT OK

# 104

"Arianna Huffington is unattractive, both inside and out.
I fully understand why her former husband left her
for a man—he made a good decision."
JEEZ, COULDN'T HE AT LEAST HAVE LEFT OUT THE SEX PART?

# 105

BOEHNER WAS WRONG:
*TRUMP* IS LUCIFER IN THE FLESH

# 106

DOCTORS HAVE DISCOVERED A NEW CATEGORY
OF MENTAL ILLNESS:
VOTING FOR TRUMP

# 107

HEY, TRUMP ISN'T ALL BAD
HE'S DESTROYED THE REPUBLICAN PARTY

# 108

TRUMP IS THE MOST UNLOVABLE MAN
THE UNIVERSE HAS EVER CONSPIRED TO PRODUCE

# 109

AND YOU THOUGHT MITT ROMNEY WAS BAD!

# 110

AARON JAMES DEFINES AN ASSHOLE
AS SOMEONE WHO PISSES ON THE CARPET
TO GAIN ATTENTION
TRUMP PISSES ON EVERYTHING AND EVERYONE
TO GAIN ATTENTION

# III

TRUMP PRESENTS AN EXTRAORDINARY
METAPHYSICAL PROBLEM
. . . OR IS HE JUST AN ORDINARY SHITHEAD?

# 112

LET'S JUST PUT IT THIS WAY:
I'M NOT GOING TO VOTE FOR TRUMP

# 113

TRUMP SAYS OBAMA WASN'T BORN
IN THE UNITED STATES
TRUMP WASN'T BORN ANYWHERE
HE WAS INSTIGATED

# 114

YOU DIDN'T BELIEVE THERE WERE
THAT MANY CRACKERS
WHO WOULD VOTE FOR TRUMP?
THEY ARE NOT CRACKERS
THEY ARE NIHILISTS

# 115

Honk if you think Trump is a major asshole
Honk twice if you think Trump
is a major major asshole

# 116

TRUMP'S TIES ARE ALMOST ALWAYS
LONG, WIDE AND BRIGHT RED
WISHFUL THINKING

# 117

TRUMP? AAARRRRRRRRRRGH!!!

# 118

IT'S <u>SO</u> BUMMER
WE ARE FORCED TO TAKE THIS MAN SERIOUSLY

# 119

TRUMP: OUR DESCENDENTS WILL LOOK BACK
AT THE HISTORY OF THIS TIME
WITH ABSOLUTE ASTONISHMENT
THAT THIS MAN WAS LET OUT OF HIS PLAYPEN

# 120

RUMP TRUMP

# 121

DOUBLE RUMP TRUMP

# 122

I DON'T KNOW . . . DOES TRUMP EVER
DO A GOOD THING?
DOES HE FLOSS?

# 123

TRUMP IS ACCUSED OF BEING A MISOGYNIST.
HE DENIES IT.
HE SAYS HE HAS NEVER MARRIED
ANYBODY BLACK.

# 124

IT'S NICE TO KNOW WE'RE GOING TO BE
EMBARRASSED AROUND THE WORLD
EVERY TIME TRUMP OPENS HIS MOUTH

# 125

Trump: To take seriously
an obviously pathological man
itself amounts to a pathology

# 126

DONALD TRUMP: A WORSE VERSION
OF HUGH HEFNER

# 127

DONALD TRUMP FUCKS EVERYTHING IN SIGHT
AND NOT IN SIGHT

# 128

TRUMP ACCUSES OBAMA OF BEING A MUSLIM
IT COULD GET WORSE
MITT ROMNEY COULD ACCUSE TRUMP
OF BEING A UNITARIAN

# 129

TRUMP SAYS HE FUCKS
ONLY WOMEN WHO ARE A 10
I'M NOT SURE—
CAN HE COUNT THAT HIGH?

# 130

TRUMP IS A TIT MAN
I'M A BRAIN PERSON

# 131

TRUMP: GOD'S REVENGE
FOR DOUBTING HIS EXISTENCE?

# 132

WHAT'S IT LIKE TO BE FUCKED BY TRUMP?
WE'RE ALL FINDING OUT

# 133

ROCKEFELLER FLIPPED US. TRUMP FUCKS US.

# 134

IF KNOWLEDGE IS POWER, DONALD TRUMP
IS ARNOLD STANG

# 135

HOW ABOUT THE DONALD
AS RELIABLE CUSTODIAN OF NUCLEAR WEAPONS?
RIGHT UP THERE WITH KIM JONG-UN, RIGHT?

# 136

TRUMP DOES NOT HATE THE CHINESE
MANY OF HIS FRIENDS ARE CHINESE
HE KNOWS A LOT ABOUT THE CHINESE
HE KNOWS THAT THE SLITS OF CHINESE WOMEN
DO NOT RUN SIDEWAYS AT ALL

# 137

I MEAN, WHAT'S NOT TO LIKE
ABOUT A REAL ESTATE SALESMAN AS PRESIDENT?

# 138

YOU'VE GOT A LONG WAIT:
WAITING FOR TWO CONSECUTIVE
LOGICALLY-CONNECTED SENTENCES
TO COME OUT OF TRUMP'S MOUTH

# 139

WHAT DOES TRUMP'S CANDIDACY SIGNIFY?
JUST THE FUTURE BREAKDOWN
OF THE AMERICAN SYSTEM OF GOVERNMENT

# 140

TRUMP ON BOARD. CRASH INTO ME!!

# 141

TO THE DUMBASS GOP:
YOU ASKED FOR HIM, YOU GOT HIM

# 142

Momma said there would be days like this.
No way.
Trump was not within her horizon.
(Or anybody's.)

# 143

Let us now praise famous men.
Trump excepted.

# 144

TRUMP IS LIKE POISON IVY:
SCRATCHING IT MAKES IT WORSE

# 145

TRUMP IS LIKE AIDS:
CHRONIC AND INCURABLE

## 146

TRUMP IS TO THE MEDIA
AS ABSINTHE IS TO THE ADDICT:
AN IRRESISTIBLE INDULGENCE
WHICH IS INSIDIOUSLY FATAL

# 147

I DO LIKE TRUMP TOWER—
SO KITSCHY, WHICH I LOVE

# 148

Trump: Is there really anything wrong
with having a President
who's stupider than the guy next door?

# 149

WHEN WAS THE LAST TIME YOU WERE ASKED
TO VOTE FOR AN ASSHOLE FOR PRESIDENT?

# 150

Are the voters who vote for Trump
really despicable persons?
Oh, no, not all. On the average.

# 151

To give political power to someone (Trump) who does not know how political power is exercised is criminal

# 152

A part of me wants Trump to win.
We need to have Trump to kick around more.

# 153

Now and forever let every entity
with the Trump name on it
be stricken, wither and die

# 154

I DON'T KNOW . . . I LIKED PATAKI

# 155

If any Republican fails to denounce Trump, they lose forever any claim to respectability, if that should particularly matter to them

# 156

I PREFER PEOPLE WHO ARE NOT CAPTURED
—BY AN ASSHOLE

# 157

EVERY SECOND WE ARE FORCED
TO PAY ATTENTION TO TRUMP
IS A DEAD LOSS

# 158

ABT. ANYBODY BUT TRUMP. I MEAN IT.

# 159

I GUESS TRUMP DYES HIS FACE
WITH FAKE SUNTAN
BECAUSE HE THINKS AMERICANS ARE TOO WHITE

# 160

I DON'T KNOW
IT JUST GIVES ME PAIN
TO SEE THIS FUCKER SUCCEED

# 161

ONE IS PREPARED TO MAKE SOME ALLOWANCES
FOR A PERSON
BUT TRUMP IS RIDICULOUS

# 162

Trump: "Norman Vincent ('The Power of Positive Thinking') Peale was my pastor." Have we here the explanation of The Donald's relentlessly, unexceptionally positive nature?

# 163

"THE BEAUTY OF ME (TRUMP) IS THAT I'M VERY RICH."
INDEED, ASK HIS WIVES.

# 164

THE ENGLISH FUCKED UP. LET'S NOT.

# 165

FUCK TRUMP AND THE AIRPLANE HE RODE IN ON

# 166

IT'S NOT THAT TRUMP IS A SIMPLETON,
A VULGARIAN
A BULLY, A CHEAT, A FRAUD AND A LIAR
IT'S THAT HE'S A JERK

# 167

TRUMP VERY UNFORTUNATELY
SUFFERS FROM
THE UNIQUELY DISTRESSING COMBINATION OF
EXTREME IGNORANCE AND EXTREME NASTINESS

# 168

Pennsylvanians!
You are asked to interrupt
your animal and spousal abuse
long enough to vote for Trump.
Is the sacrifice worth it?

# 169

PUTIN SAYS TRUMP IS INTELLIGENT
DOES THIS GIVE YOU REASSURANCE?

# 170

TRUMP SAYS "MAJORLY"
WHEN HE MEANS "MAJOR LEAGUE"
SO WE CAN SAY THAT HE IS A "MAJORLY CREEP"

# 171

PLEASE, GOD, LET TRUMP WIN
MY BUMPERS ARE WAITING

# 172

TRUMP:
SHIT, CHARLES MANSON HAS MORE APPEAL

# 173

2000 YEARS OF CHRISTIAN CIVILIZATION
AND THE END PRODUCT IS TRUMP?
I THINK I'LL BECOME A MUSLIM

# 174

WOULD A TRUMP PRESIDENCY
BE MORE CATASTROPHIC OR HUMOROUS?

# 175

WHAT'S NOT TO LIKE ABOUT TRUMP?
GOT A WEEK, I'LL TELL YOU

## 176

IF TRUMP WINS AND IS INAUGURATED
THE NEXT DAY
HE WILL QUIT AND SAY IT WAS ALL A JOKE

# 177

TRUMP:
"WHAT THE FUCK IS GOING ON?
I ONLY WANTED
TO GET MY NAME IN THE PAPER."

# 178

I LIKE TRUMP
VULGARITY RUNS IN MY FAMILY

# 179

MAY ONE SAY WHAT SHOULD BE SAID?
FUCK TRUMP

# 180

THEY ASKED TRUMP WHAT HE THOUGHT OF MISOGYNY
HE ASKED IF SHE HAD BIG TITS

# 181

Q. Why didn't Trump qualify for the draft?
A. Trump didn't qualify for the draft because he is daft.

# 182

TRUMP IS TEACHING AMERICANS THAT TO BE
INCOHERENT, STUPID AND VULGAR IS OK
BUT WE ALREADY KNEW THAT, DIDN'T WE?

# 183

TENANTS IN TRUMP'S APARTMENTS
SAY THEY ARE NOT AS WELL CONSTRUCTED
AS HIS HAIRDO

# 184

TRUMP IS THE REDUCTIO AD ADSURDUM OF DEMOCRACY
NO
TRUMP IS THE REDUCTIO AD ABSURDUM
OF HUMAN EXISTENCE

# 185

TRUMP & TRUTH: NOT FOUND AT THE SAME PLACE

# 186

TRUMP: A POLITICAL OUTLIAR

# 187

TRUMP: NO HOW, NO WAY

# 188

TRUMP IS THE ALTERNATIVE CANDIDATE
ALTERNATIVE TO SANITY

## 189

THE WORLD'S MOST SUPERFLUOUS PERSON:
A POLITICAL ATTACK DOG FOR DONALD TRUMP

# 190

"TWO CORINTHIANS, RIGHT?"

# 191

TRUMP IS THE ONLY KNOWN
REAL ESTATE DEVELOPER
TO BUILD A BUILDING IN THE SHAPE OF A VULVA
(TRUMP OCEAN CLUB TOWER, PANAMA CITY)

# 192

Trump says avoiding STDs was his Vietnam War.
We did lose the Vietnam War.
Do we hope that he fared better?

# 193

Trump: "more Presidential" = less of a shit. Impossible.

# 194

I REALLY RESENT HAVING TO USE MY BUMPER SPACE
TO PERSUADE YOU HOW BAD TRUMP IS

# 195

IT'S IMPOSSIBLE TO BE INFINITELY SHITTY
NO, IT'S TRUMP

# 196

IF THEY GAVE ASSHOLES RANKS
TRUMP WOULD BE ASSHOLE-IN-CHIEF

# 197

"Trump, Giuliani, Christy."
"Why did you have to say that?
Now I've lost my appetite."

# 198

TRUMP SAYS HE'S AN OUTSIDER
FOR GOD'S SAKE, DON'T LET THE BASTARD IN

# 199

TRUMP: HE FAVORS FAMILY VALUES
CORLEONE FAMILY VALUES

# 200

LET'S MAKE TRUMP THE "WINNER" A LOSER

# 201

It is truly almost impossible to conceive
how a single individual (Trump)
can accumulate so many bad qualities

# 202

THEY SAY THAT HILLARY IS NOT LIKEABLE
COMPARED TO TRUMP SHE IS
THE EPITOME OF LOVABILITY

# 203

There is a word that very well describes Trump but that one has not yet seen applied to him. Let's apply it: he's a prick.

# 204

RICH PEOPLE DON'T LIKE YOU
THIS INCLUDES TRUMP

# 205

WILL THERE BE ANY HISPANICS WHO VOTE FOR TRUMP?
YES
ONE SUPPOSES THERE WERE A FEW JEWS WHO VOTED
FOR HITLER

# 206

IF TRUMP WEREN'T RICH HE'D BE LOCKED UP

# 207

THE EVOLUTION OF THE REPUBLICAN PARTY:
FROM LINCOLN TO TRUMP:
FROM THE SUBLIME TO THE RIDICULOUS

# 208

"TRUMPY" MEANS PLUMP AND NASTY

# 209

THE TIME WE REALLY HAVE TO WORRY
ABOUT IMMIGRATION
IS WHEN FEWER PEOPLE WANT TO IMMIGRATE IN
THAN IMMIGRATE OUT

# 210

TRUMP: AN EVIL TWIN WITHOUT A TWIN

# 211

LET'S SAY SOMETHING GOOD ABOUT TRUMP:
HE'S NOT A DRUNK
(AS FAR AS WE KNOW)

# 212

IF YOU THINK TRUMP WOULD BE GOOD FOR YOU
I'VE GOT SOME SARSAPARILLA I'D LIKE TO SELL YOU

# 213

THE REPUBLICAN PARTY WILL NEVER RECOVER
FROM INFLICTING THIS MAN ON US

# 214

A TRUMP VOTER:
THE DEFINITION OF POLITICALLY CHALLENGED

# 215

AT LEAST WE CAN INSULT TRUMP WITHOUT BEING SHOT.
SO FAR.

# 216

Give us a break, Trump. Vanish.

# 217

Can we hope that a limit on the damage
Trump can do
is set by his stupidity?

## 218

Trump's national finance chair is Steven Mnuchin.
Trump dwarf-tosses?

# 219

TRUMP SAYS IT'S NOT TRUE
HE DOESN'T KNOW ANYTHING ABOUT FOREIGN AFFAIRS
HE SAYS HE'S HAD LOTS OF AFFAIRS WITH FOREIGNERS

## 220

TRUMP SAYS HE'S OK WITH TORTURE
OBVIOUSLY, SINCE THAT'S WHAT IT IS
TO HAVE TO LISTEN TO HIM TALK

# 221

HOW CAN A GUY 70 YEARS OLD BE SO UNAWARE?

# 222

IT IS NOT TOO EASY TO BECOME RICH
BUT TRUMP SHOWS
IT IS TOO EASY FOR IDIOTS TO BECOME RICH

# 223

THE ROAD TRUMP TAKES IS SO LOW
IT'S UNDERGROUND

## 224

THERE IS THE GREATEST GENERATION AND THEN
THERE IS THE UNGREATEST INDIVIDUAL (TRUMP)

# 225

HEY, TRUMP, GIVE IT UP,
YOU'RE DAMAGING YOUR BRAND
NOBODY WANTS TO RENT A PROPERTY
WITH THE NAME OF A DIPSHIT ON IT

## 226

IF DONALD TRUMP CAN DO THE JOB OF PRESIDENT
MY ASSHOLE CAN DO THE JOB OF GOD

# 227

TRUMP IS TO A THINKER
AS A SHITEATER IS TO A GOURMAND

# 228

A FART MAKES MORE SENSE THAN TRUMP

# 229

FOR SOME REASON TRUMP'S EFFORTS
TO GIVE GREED A GOOD NAME FALL SHORT

# 230

NOT GETTING THE CLAP WAS TRUMP'S VIETNAM
HIS ELECTION WOULD
BE OUR ARMAGEDDON

# 231

Gaydon Carter calls Trump
a "short-fingered vulgarian."
Let's contemplate having
a "short-fingered vulgarian" President.

## 232

YOU KNOW, IT MAY NOT BE A GOOD IDEA
TO HAVE A PRESIDENT
WITH A PERSONALITY DISORDER

# 233

DRUMPF? HRUMPF!

# 234

There's nothing wrong with Trump—he's a perfect idiot

# 235

Donald Trump's success shows
just how low standards are in the private sector

# 236

TRUMP, ARE YOU REALLY SUCH AN ALPHA GUY?
SHOW US YOUR TAX RETURNS AND YOUR COCK

# 237

Gee, what could it be about Trump
that makes me a little doubtful?

# 238

Trump says: "I know more about ISIS
than the generals do. Believe me."
We don't.

# 239

Sorry, folks, I'm just too intelligent to vote for Trump

# 240

Hate to tell you yahoos: Trump is Establishment

# 241

SCIENCE HAS YET
TO OFFER AN EXPLANATION
FOR THE EXISTENCE OF DONALD J. TRUMP

# 242

NATURE HAS YET TO OFFER AN EXCUSE
FOR ALLOWING THE EXISTENCE OF DONALD J. TRUMP

# 243

TRUMP IS NOT POLITICALLY CORRECT
NOT CULTURALLY CORRECT
NOT MENTALLY CORRECT

## 244

A VERY SUBLE PRINCIPLE THAT MAY BE ESCAPING TRUMP:
IF YOU INSULT PEOPLE
THEY MAY NOT WISH TO VOTE FOR YOU

# 245

TRUMP'S FATHER WAS AN ANCHOR BABY

# 246

MY CAT OSCAR KNOWS BETTER
THAN TO VOTE FOR TRUMP
DO YOU?

# 247

Trump:
"I would build a great wall, and nobody builds walls better than me, believe me, and I'll build them very inexpensively."
Naw—he'd subcontract to the Chinese.
They have experience building a Great Wall
and are cheaper.

## 248

TRUMP
NOT CIVIL
NOT CIVILIZED

## 249

You may not regret Hillary losing
but you sure as hell would regret Trump winning

# 250

WARNING!
DICKHEAD (TRUMP) ON THE LOOSE

# 251

TO BE AN DISRUPTOR
IS ONE THING
TO BE A DESTROYER OF REASON
IS ANOTHER

# 252

TRUMP = LOSING!

# 253

I should vote for a nut?
To this I say Nuts!

## 254

THE KOCH BROTHERS ARE WORKING
TO RECONSTITUTE THE REPUBLICAN PARTY
DESTROYED BY TRUMP
GOOD LUCK WITH THAT

# 255

TRUMP HAS WRITTEN A NEW BOOK:
"THE ART OF THE STEAL"

# 256

THE WHITE HOUSE IS NOT
A PARTICULARLY GOOD VENUE
TO DEMONSTRATE YOUR ASSHOLE QUALITIES

# 257

BORIS JOHNSON IS ALSO A DEMAGOGUE
BUT HE CAN SPEAK LATIN AND GREEK
AND QUOTES SHAKESPEARE

# 258

I could vote for Trump, yes
but—you know—there is self-respect involved

# 259

Trump would turn the American government
into a reality TV show—
a virtual reality TV show

# 260

How easily Trump has effected
the collapse of Conservative Republicanism!
His only good deed!

# 261

ONLY CHUMPS
VOTE TRUMP

# 262

WE LIVE IN AN HISTORICAL TIME
THE REPUBLICAN CANDIDATE FOR PRESIDENT
IS THE CREEPIEST CANDIDATE FOR PRESIDENT
IN AMERICAN HISTORY

# 263

The first rule of political science:
a creep should not be elected President

# 264

The only reason the word asshole was invented
was because they knew that someday
there would be Donald J. Trump

# 265

Please, somebody edit Trump's DNA
to produce something resembling a human being

# 266

If you think we have to take a lot from Trump,
think of what poor Melania has to take from him

# 267

I have no trouble with the fact
that a lot of people like Trump.
I am reassured that I am more intelligent
than so many people.

# 268

A TRUMP PRESIDENCY MIGHT BE WORTH IT
FOR THE AMUSEMENT IT WOULD PROVIDE.
OR NOT.

# 269

Trump should not be faulted
for his complete lack of a sense of reality.
There are a lot of people like that.

# 270

PENCE UNWISE AND TRUMP FOOLISH

# 271

Wikipedia says Trump's wife is a Slovene-American jewelry and watch designer and former model. I'd say that makes her better qualified to be President than hubby.

# 272

"I could stand in the middle of 5th Avenue
and shoot somebody and it wouldn't lose voters."
True to the extent that whoever in the City
you chose to shoot wasn't going to vote for you.

# 273

RATHER A COMMUNIST IN THE WHITE HOUSE
THAN A NARCISSIST

# 274

The funny part about all this
is that there just might exist
the possibility that this shitsky could win

# 275

I DON'T LOVE MY COCK
MORE THAN TRUMP LOVES HIMSELF

## 276

If you are close enough to read this
and intend to vote for Trump
you are a tailgater and should be shot

# 277

DUMP ON TRUMP

# 278

I AIN'T WITH HIM

# 279

THERE'S ABNORMAL
AND THEN THERE'S TRUMP ABNORMAL

# 280

What Trump really means is:
"Let's make America straight again."

# 281

THERE'S ALWAYS SOMETHING
THAT SEEMS TO BE ANNOYING TRUMP
MAYBE HIS BUTTPLUG DOESN'T FIT

# 282

We are feeling very sorry for the Republicans for making such a horrific mistake

# 283

TRUMP FOR PRESIDENT
AND THE THREE STOOGES FOR CABINET

## 284

I serve with Vladimir Putin.
I know Vladimir Putin.
Vladimir Putin is a friend of mine.
Donald, you're no Vladimir Putin.

# 285

IT IS THE AGE OF ANTI-ENLIGHTENMENT

# 286

ASSHOLES DON'T ALWAYS WIN

# 287

REPUBLICANS ARE SO SENSITIVE
JUST BECAUSE SOMEBODY CAME
AND DESTROYED THEIR PARTY

## 288

SOMETHING MUST HAVE BEEN AMISS
WITH THE YOUNG DONALD TRUMP
HE WAS RICH AND DIDN'T GO TO HARVARD

# 289

And Trump does not have a natural constituency
in other assholes
as every asshole despises the other assholes
as much as everybody else does

# 290

Everybody loves Trump:
isn't he just so lovable?
A little vicious maybe . . .

# 291

TRUMP:
FULL OF HIMSELF
FULL OF IT

## 292

NOT EVEN GOD LOVES TRUMP MORE THAN TRUMP

# 293

LISTENING TO TRUMP TALK
IS LIKE LISTENING TO A LUNATIC
THERE IS A REASON FOR THIS

# 294

Trump could be worse
though that is unlikely

# 295

HOW DOTH TRUMP OFFEND ME?
LET ME COUNT THE WAYS . . .

# 296

I get it. They're going to vote for the person
least competent to run the Government
by way of destroying the Government.
Well, ain't that the cat's meow?

# 297

TRUMP: THE DON RICKLES OF POLITICS
EXCEPT THAT TRUMP'S INSULT SCHTICK
ISN'T FUNNY

## 298

PEOPLE WONDER WHAT TRUMP
WOULD DO IN THE WHITE HOUSE
PRIVATIZE IT AND CONVERT IT TO CONDOS?

# 299

Trump: Would you trust this man
with your daughter?
The federal budget, maybe?

# 300

WATCHING TRUMP PERFORM
IS LIKE WATCHING
YOUR DIRTY OL' UNCLE MORTY EXPOSE HIMSELF

# 301

Trump's last hairdresser quit
saying, "It has become too ambitious a project.
It has become beyond my capacity."

# 302

WHEN TRUMP DIES
HIS HAIR WILL BE DONATED
TO RIPLEY'S BELIEVE IT OR NOT

# 303

IN TRUMP'S CASE, CHARACTER ANALYSIS
IS IMPOSSIBLE
THERE IS NO CHARACTER THERE

## 304

AMERICA CAN DO BETTER
THAN ELECT AN ASSHOLE AS PRESIDENT
(IT HAD BETTER DO BETTER)

# 305

Q. Name the one word that has never been associated with Donald J. Trump and never will be.

A. Empathy.

# 306

PUSSYEATING DOESN'T WORK FOR TRUMP
IF SHE MUSSES HIS HAIRDO

# 307

THE REASON TRUMP IS REPULSIVE
TO SO MANY PEOPLE
IS THAT HE IS SO REPULSIVE

# 308

TRUMP SAYS 2ND AMENDMENTERS
MIGHT SHOOT HILLARY
WHOA! NOT THE PATH OF WISDOM
FOR DONALD J. TRUMP TO BROACH THE SUBJECT
OF ASSASSINATION OF PRESIDENTIAL CANDIDATES

# 309

WHAT IS IT ABOUT ME
THAT I DON'T APPRECIATE TRUMP?
BEING SANE DOESN'T HELP

## 310

In 2012 Aaron James wrote a book on assholes:
"Assholes: A Theory"
In 2016 he felt compelled to write a supplement just on Trump:
"Assholes: A Theory of Donald Trump"

# 311

TRUMP DOES NOT HATE NIGGRAS
TRUMP LOVES NIGGRAS
SOME OF HIS BEST MAIDS HAVE BEEN NIGGRAS
HE MAY EVEN HAVE FUCKED A COUPLE

# 312

TRUMP:
SOON TO BE THE BIGGEST LOSER
THE WORLD HAS EVER KNOWN
(FINGERS CROSSED)

# 313

YOU'LL NOTICE TRUMP PROPOSES NO SERIOUS POLICIES
ON ANYTHING
THEY COME LATER, AFTER THE ELECTION
TRUST HIM

# 314

OCCASIONALLY SOMEONE WILL TELL TRUMP
TO FUCK HIMSELF
HE WOULD IF HE COULD

# 315

IT IS BORING TO ALWAYS BE TALKING ABOUT
TRUMP'S DEFECTS
BUT THEY ARE ALWAYS THERE
STARING YOU IN THE FACE

# 316

FIRST JOCK ITCH AND NOW TRUMP

# 317

IS TRUMP NECESSARY?

# 318

AS A POLITICIAN TRUMP IS NOT ALL BAD:
HE DRESSES WELL

# 319

TRUMP SAYS HE'S RELIGIOUS
HE SAYS GOD MEETS WITH HIM
EVERY ONCE IN A WHILE
HE SAYS THEY GET ALONG VERY WELL

# 320

GOD AND TRUMP ARE ON A FIRST-NAME BASIS
TRUMP CALLS GOD "LORDY"
GOD CALLS TRUMP "SCREWBALL"

# 321

TRUMP WOULD APPOINT WHO TO THE SUPREME COURT?
RUDY GIULIANI?  NEWT GINGRICH?  DON KING?

# 322

TRUMP CAN'T CONCEIVE OF THE WORLD
WITHOUT HIMSELF
NOBODY ELSE HAS A PROBLEM WITH DOING THAT

# 323

When Trump dies he will be embalmed and preserved like Lenin
and put on permanent display in the lobby of Trump Tower
by the souvenir shop

# THE AUTHOR

*Painting by Marcia Flammonde*

John Wirth is a gay nudist and is the author
of *Stories of That Time*
and the editor of *Gay Doggerel*

www.ingramcontent.com/pod-product-compliance
Lightning Source LLC
Chambersburg PA
CBHW060835280326
41934CB00007B/792